T0194941

IF I'D ONLY
KNOWN
THEN
WHAT I
KNOW NOW

CHARLES JOHNSON

authorHOUSE®

AuthorHouse™
1663 Liberty Drive
Bloomington, IN 47403
www.authorhouse.com
Phone: 1 (800) 839-8640

Published by AuthorHouse 06/12/2019

ISBN: 978-1-7283-1563-8 (sc)
ISBN: 978-1-7283-1562-1 (e)

Library of Congress Control Number: 2019907576

Print information available on the last page.

This book is printed on acid-free paper.

How many times have you heard this saying from people you know? And from people you don't know? For some of you, you may not have ever heard this saying but a lot of you have. I have heard this saying many times from people I knew. The sad thing about it is, many of those people have passed away. But some of them are still living today. When you hear someone say this, it is because they have done some things in his or her life that they are not pleased with their life they care for and if they had the chance to do it over. They could do it difference they would do it the right way. I am one of those people who said if I knew then what I know now, my life would be much better. The only good thing about my past life is God was with me. See I have always known God baptized at a young age. My grandmother told me all about God. Although she told me I still took some dark road in went the wrong way. But never forgot about God. And what she teaches me about God. Proverbs 22:6 say *Train up a child in the way he should go. And when he is old, he will not depart from it.* One thing for sure God have never depart from me. I feel that the world children don't know enough about God. There are who know and have heard about God but that not all.

My grandmother, who I call big mommy, took me to church with her when she went. She didn't go to church every Sunday. But she did go and she believe in God. While my brother and sister would be on the outside playing, I would be in the house with big mommy. Whatever she did, I was there. When she went fishing, I was there. When she went to the grocery store, I was there. I knew I was big mommy's favorite grandson. Because she would let me get away with stuff that she didn't let my other brother and sister get away with. But I knew how far I could go. And I never test her. I remember one day when big mommy went to work, my mother came down to the where we were living with big mommy. My mother lives up the street from us with my other brother and sister. They were all the youngest my mother keeps them with her. And the four oldest big mommies raise us. When I was a boy, I was told almost everything. I remember one time she told me if I could feed myself I could feed one more person I never forgot that. She also told, "Son be careful about the woman you get together with and always treat the woman well." She also said, "A nickel in your hand is worth more than a thousand in the bush." In other word, what's in your hand, you got it, it is yours. Never leave what you have for something ease because you don't know what you may get." She told me to be a good man and treat everyone you meet with respect. It would be good for a woman to meet a good man. And a man of God is as good as they come a worldly man is like the devil. He sees to deceive the woman. He is the same as the serpent. He is the serpent in human flesh and the beginning of Satan use the snake body and for years. He uses the man body to do his dirty work. Remember, God was and is a spirit and he sent son into the world for man say. And when His son came into world, He took on human flesh. And before Satan was put out of heaven, he too was spirit he is the ruled of this world and I think because he was here on the earth before Jesus God son His only Son, he has son led way and one of his led way is to use man and getting him to sin. This is the woman need a Godly man to let you know a real man of God Satan cannot live in this man. But he will temp and test this man. But the man of God knows what to do to get the devil to flee his. The woman needs to know a man of God he is always on track. He will have his bad moment but he will know what to do. This man is led by God and he will do the right thing a woman needed this kind of man this man will make a good husband, and a good family man. He knows the way. They say a happy wife. A happy husband. A woman looks for the man to make her happy, who is not perfect but the man of God will be happy in every way because he knows his God is perfect. He has no need to worry. The woman disobeys her husband in the beginning of time. The woman said to the serpent we may eat the fruit of the trees of the garden, but of the fruit of the tree which is in the midst of the garden, God has said you shall not eat it, nor shall you touch it lest you die. Genesis 3:2, God never said this to the woman. And how do I know this because if God had said this to the woman there would have been no reason for the woman to have giving Adam the fruit because her eye would have been open the minute, she ate of the tree that God told Adam not to eat of. A woman needs to know that a man is like a roaring lion. She needs to be sober, be vigilant because her adversary the man walks about like a roaring lion, seeking whom he may devour.

The woman should resist the man. She should steadfast in the faith and wait on the Lord. To give her a husband, and when she gets a husband from the Lord, he will take care of her. He will treat her right he will take care of her, the man of God, he always knows if don't he will answered to God, if the woman let the man do what God put him into the world to do, she will be a happy woman.

The man is to led the way. God never mint for a woman to led the way. The man is the rule over the woman. Genesis 3:16 to the woman, He said, "I will greatly multiply your sorrow and your conception; in pain you shall bring forth children; your desire shall be for your husband, and he shall rule over you." It seems like the woman want to rule the world and anyone who know God, He is not going to let that happen. The woman needs to get that in her head and when she does, it will be a much better life for her. She needs to know how bad a man get God will never turn from man who He created and what He put him in the world to do. God is a perfect, God don't any mistake. Like I said, God will never replace man with woman. If He did that than everything, He did He would have made many mistakes and we all know that this not true. He is perfect. God knew man before He created him. That is one of good things about God. He knew that man would not hold up and that he would not obey Him, it is so important for a woman to be patient and wait on the Lord. Man and woman think it okay? With God to mistreat each and that God will take their side. The man is worried about putting on the same as man he is a mess up. This is what man wants, but not with God. What God wants is to treat people right. Man is to love his wife. And do her right. Some woman is so mean to their husband it is a shame on her. And the bad thing about, it she doesn't care about his feeling. When a woman is done, she is done. So then, why want she move on some of them do move. Other wants to stay around just to take the through hell. It not fair but she doesn't give a shit. Any man who want to be around scorned woman that must be out of his mind. A scorned woman has no feeling in her action. When she come, she put out and say whatever in her mind and heart.

A scorned woman has no color, no age and they all can become a scorned woman if she is push to the limit. Her heart turns to ice and she less likely to forgive or forget. Punishment is all on her mind and the only thing someone can do, is get out of her way and far from her. I have deal with a number of scorned women and I can tell you it was not easy, it was like hell. A good man almost all the time get used when he is in a relationship. The say she looking for a good man but when she finds one, she says he is good but. There go that but he is good but. And when we say but we open the door for doubts. And when we doubt, trouble come in. In just like that it ends before it starts. The woman has her doubt but she doesn't say no. She believes she can change the man and when she cannot. She put herself in the position to become a scorned woman. All she had to do was say no and move on with her life. Only God can change a person and it has to be if the person wants to be change. a woman needs to understand this and If she does, she saves herself pains and scuffing. The woman believe she have so much love that she can change anyone. And with her thinking like this, she brings trouble to herself. God always warned human when things are not right. But the human doesn't want the warning from God because they think they know more than God. That is a big mistake for anyone to think they know more than God, the one who created them. Take the time out and think about what God did when He created the world. He did something that no other could possible do. And there are some people who say there is no God. Any man who say there is no God, that men is a fool. How can anyone look at the world and say there is no God, if someone over 2000 years ago would have told me about a rainbow that He set in the sky and some 2000 years later, that rainbow would be seem in the sky after it rain and it put there to remind the people what God said what would happen. How could I believe there is no God? How anyone say this if he didn't know what he was talking about. Genesis 9:13, "*I set my rainbow in the cloud, and it shall be for the sign the covenant between me and the earth.*" Some people want others to believe there is no God.

I grew up old school. Meaning, any old people in the neighbor saw me during something wrong they had permission to beat my ass and when I got home, I would get another beating. Maybe them was the good days when I was a young boy, I was the neighbor good old boy. I help out many of the old people in the neighborhood, when I sports with the other boy and we pick teams who ever did the picking they wanted me on their team I was that good. And I remember I was a bad ass. I was a good person but a bad ass. If I know then what I know now I would not have been a bad ass what the difference time make. But I was young and I didn't know what I know now. But thanks be to God better He who is in me than he who is in the world. I never mistreat anyone that I remember. And if I have, I have asked the Lord to forgive me. And I ask Him to forgive me from my heart. If people would just treat everyone, they met like a stranger the world would be a better place. Exodus 22:21, *"You shall neither mistreat a stranger nor oppress him, for you were stranger in the land of Egypt."* My big mom always told me not to mistreat a stranger. And the reason for that was because you don't them. When man is a man of God, he will know how to treat a woman. He will be a gentleman to the woman, but woman must carry herself in the way a woman should carry herself. It would help if the woman was a woman of God. It is not easy for man and woman to be together in marriage if one of them is not with God, both man and woman must have faith in God. A man need to pray and he need to believe and he need to do. I must say, I pray all the time. I thank God all the time for all He does for me. And what He has done for me, man just don't know what he missing out on when he doesn't have God in his or her life. God knows the way because He is the way and how good it is to have someone who know the way to be in front leading the way. God is the one and His word mean a lot.

When I was a boy, I was good but as I got old, I seem to get in trouble more. Remember I went to jail. In when I went in front of the judge, He asked what was going on with me. Every time his count door open, he sees me. All I could say to the judge was that, "Judge if you let me go home, you will never see me again." The judge told me that he was going to let me go home, and he said to me that if he see me again, he was going to send me to prison. I said to the judge, "You will never see mean again." That over 40 years and the judge never saw me again today. And the reason for that was I didn't want to go to prison. Just many other men who go to jail make up his mind to stay out of trouble he can. All he needed to do tell himself he not going to get in any trouble. Just because he a child of God it does not mean he will not get in trouble.

I recalled work with the correctional office. My job was to oversee inmates. I remember one day before I went to work, I stop by the part to get a little rest and while I was setting in my SUV, I would lower the window halfway down and I fell asleep. One of the inmates came up to the SUV I was in and he just stood looking at me while I was sleeping. When I open my eyes, I saw him standing there and ask him why he was standing there. He said to me that he had been there for a while. He told me that if he didn't like me. He would have cut my throat. He said the other inmates respect me for during my job and that I treated all the inmate the same way and that I didn't have no favor one they like that. I would tell all of them just because I was out of prison that didn't mean anything. I told them that I could be in there place tomorrow. And that was true. I would tell all of them to go out and find a job and be a man. I told them that a man who didn't have a job that didn't want anything out of life. The world is full of sin and as long as men live, he will sin and he will pay for it. I try to do the right thing but I didn't try very hard. Every time I try, something got in my way. I got a job with the department of correction so I could help the men and jail. Then I became a volunteer youth coach and for 17 years, I coach young men with the police department and with city rec park. I was a good coach but one of the young men on the team I was coaching got killed. He came home from church when a tow truck driver hit the car he was in from the rear. The tow driver was racing to get to another car accident. The night before the accident, the young man and I went to a football banquet so that all the boy in the sport league can receive their award for playing in the sport program. The very next day, that young man was killed. A day after his death, someone was knocking on my door early in the morning. When I opened the door, I knew person who was knocking she told me that her mom who was the young man who was killed she wanted to see me and when I got to her home. She told me her son was killed on Sunday. I remember the young man was killed my asst coach and I was standing in his front yard talking like we always do. We saw the police and the fire truck and ambulance going down the street, I said to my asst coach something bad might happen down the street but we continue to talk and we were talking about our player and how good that played the game. We didn't know it was one of our player who was killed. All this happen in Sunday morning.

Later that day, I was on my way out so look down the street where the accident was so I walk down to the seam of the accident to see what happen. When I got there, I saw a man standing by and asked him what happened. He told me that a kid was killed in the accident he didn't know who the kid was. All he knew a young boy was killed. This was a good kid. I asked his mom what happy she told me that her son left church to come see her before she had to go back to the rehab center. When I first met

Jr, he as walking down the street going home, I asked him if he liked football, he said yes. I asked him if he wants to play for me since I have a team. He said yes but his mom won't let him play. I told him to let me talk to his mom to ask her and allow him to play for me and he said yes. I talk to his mom and she said she didn't know because she did not want her baby to get hurt. I told her he would not get hurt and that I would see to that at the time I told her that I didn't know how I would keep him from getting hurt. But told her that any way. She said ok he would play. So, I got him on the team and he came out with the other boy and he was one of the best players on the team this kid was very good football player I remember we was playing a game and the team we were playing had some pretty good players and that was fast. So, I put my best on their best so we were at the end of the game and we were winning so I took Jerry out of the game but other team kept their best player on the field for the kickoff and I remember Jerry said to me, "Coach put me out there," and I said no. I told him the score was 34 to 0. We were leading with 2 minutes in the game. So, we kickoff and they returned the kickoff for a touchdown. Jerry was so mad because they score a touchdown. He said to me see I told you coach to put out there. To keep them from scoring. I said to jerry the it over he told me coach I wanted to shout them out. we went to win first place. I remember the night of the banquet I walk outside of the banquet hall jerry came outside he was yelling you won the coach of the year he was so happy for me. He asks me could he have it. my award now all the boy who played in the program receive a trophy. I will never forget jerry he was like my own son. A friend of mind a young woman finds out the secret to controlling the minds of the world but is deceived by the love she trusts.

"I hate you, I hate you!" she screamed as she was kicking and screaming while being carried through the house. The adrenaline in her body is boiling. She said she was feeling the pounding in her head it feels like someone took a hammer and hit her on the right side of her brain. Its throbbing and I can't seem to calm down. My dad throws me into this room that's dark all black walls, no windows, no light, and one door. There is a vent on the ceiling and the only reason I know is because I feel the air coming through. Before the door closes, my dad screams out to me, you will die in here. Your life will be deleted no one will ever know you existed. Pray that God take your life because the devil is in control now. I didn't know what he meant because my brain can't quite take in the words when there is so much going on. What am I supposed to do? In here? I screamed out. Kicking the door while screaming and crying I'm bound to pass out. I'm basically blind because I have no light, I have no sight. I sit here and move my head around and try to see but truth of the matter is, it's so dark all I see is pitch black. It's so black imagine having your eyes shut with a blind fold tied around your head in a dark room while its dark outside that's how dark it is in here. I lay down and put my hands on my chest and try to hold me because I'm scared, I don't know what's going to happen to me. I need to catch breath before I have a slow death from not being able to breath. I took a short nap and is awaking by scary dream I just had. Well, it wasn't really a dream, it was a simple recollection of what happened before I was thrown in here. Walking in on my dad killing my mom. That picture will never leave my mind now that I'm in the dark, I have no choice but to remember this traumatizing thought over and over again because all I have left to do now is think I get up and try to walk around. As I walk around, I am tip toeing in small steps with my arms extended trying to find a wall or a pole or something so I can learn my way around. There are things in the room but I can't quite figure it out because I can't see what it is. I trip a few times, and touch a few things but I can't see, I can only feel. Since this place will be my new home now, all I can do is take the time out to find out what and where everything in this room is. I never thought I would be blind but now I'm blind when I can see I feel like giving up now and I haven't been in here a whole day yet. I'm in a dark room and all I can do is basically sit here until someone save me or until I die, all I can is try to survive day to day.

While I'm thinking these thoughts, the little door opens and it's a tray of. I crawl towards the light I saw for a quick second and reach out for the tray. I pick it up and set it on my lap. I'm feeling everything to figure out what it is. It's cold, somethings are mushy, somethings are hard, and somethings are rough. Its fruit. I have apples, oranges, grapes, pineapples. Peaches, strawberries, watermelon, cantaloupe, and raisins. This is weird but I'll take it. As I'm eating, so many thoughts are going through my mind, it's hard to concentrate on just one thing. A lot just happened in my life just a while ago and I can't quite grasp it. Right about now, I do want to die just so I don't have to deal with the pain anymore. I feel like my heart was snatched out of my chest and I'm left on earth with no love to give or feel. I feel like I will be alone forever and I won't ever experience love again. In this little time, I'm in this dark place I'm already turning to the dark side. I guess that's what Jason meant. Jason is my father and I want to erase the thought of him being my dad. He is now my enemy. Before he closes to the door, he said the devil is in control now and in this little time I feel like I'm being possessed for now angry I am. The floor is so hard. All I feel is my back aching and my butt falling asleep. How long will I be here? God save me, Please. I was outside playing when I heard a loud scream come out from the window. Amanda, Amanda run away. Run. I dropped my dolls and ran into the house. If I knew then what I know now my life would be better. It not too late now but it a long road back. I went upstairs into parent bedroom and my mom and dad were nowhere to be found. I stand still to see if I can hear a noise and I hear. Amanda, I need someone else. Tell God that I was ready for you to go. Being on the good side in not welcomed in this world anymore I run into the basement and seem my dad wrestling with my mom. I grab the wooden stick and un towards my father but before I can hit him, he snapped my mother neck and grab the stick from my hand and attack me with it. As I'm lying on the ground feeling the pain, he picks me up and throw me into the dungeon. I call it that because that's what it feels like. My dad is the president of a big company and my mom is a doctor. My dad called her the first lady. I wonder what the story is going to be in the media when they notice that his wife and daughter was kidnapped and is nowhere to be found just stories the media get paid to say. I hate growing up in this world where my dad works for himself, I found out the secret and I can' let it be known what it is. My mom told me when I was 8 years old and told me take it to my grave. She told me not to long ago that my dad was working with the government, he and few of his coworker had a secret.

Regarding autism, the government knew all the long about it and they know where it come from the government. I remember the word my mom said to me, "Amanda, there will come a time in your life where you are going to have to fight. And it will come a time you may had to kill and pray to God that never happy." You never want to kill no one. Love is always better than hate. Love word all the time. Hate is of the devil. Love is God. Take a look around and understand the Powell of love. Love have overcome the evil of the world. Hate came to destroy the world but He who created the world had a better ideal He sent His son His only son to save the world. And His son. Did a good saving the world? His love He gave all live today. And without His love the world would be gone. If the man doesn't have love he will turn into a bad man because he will experience hate, and he will no longer know love. On this journey, you must forget God we need Him, man must go back to his heart. And that was put in him love. He must go back to being the person he was after he destroy everything that is evil. In order to do that, he must turn from evil. Pray to God for Him help, and you must never be scared. No scared man can get anywhere because that doubt in his heart. And the word of God it tells us that we should never doubt. Now God have a problem with a man having doubt. What more can be said about that man. Faith is the part the man is missing when he doesn't use it. When new I had faith I text is and I text it in a big way.

At that time, my income was about $600.00 a month and I wanted to buy a home. So I start to look for a home. I found a home and the price was $480,000 dollars I got the home I did know how I would pay for it. But I was able to pay for it for four months. It's not God's plan that I should have that house so I lost it. When I lost the house, I continued to live and it for over 13 months and I didn't pay one cent to stay there. On the day, before the day I was support moveout my wife and a baby about two months old up stair in one of the bedroom. We were looking out of the window when I saw the sheriff coming up the street and pull in the drive way and got out of the car. And when she got out of the police car, I meet her at the door she told me that the bank gave me more time to move. At the time I had no place to take my wife and two months old baby. I had no money save up. We were breaking so I call the bank. To see if how much money was in my account. I had $14,000 dollars in my account that the military had giving me for a claim I had file a while back. So, I went from no money to $14,000 dollars so I was ready to go. I may not have a place to go, but I have money to take them somewhere. God is good. And he good all the time. I said it and I say it again God is good and He good all the time. And anyone say difference they are a fool. God maybe I secret, but his work is open to the world. The power of God. There is none like it.

Before the light come on God, is there. And before the light go out, He is there. Before the lightly. God is there. Man should never go to bed before he prays to God and he should never get up and the morning and go on his way before he prays to God, give God some love everyday he wakes up. Because if it was not for God where would man be. I say man but I'm speaking about man and woman. You believe that God wake you up in the morning you think you should not thank Him. People live one day. People die one day. But God live forever. I am blessed in my early 60s, I have grand and great grand. Thanks be to God, how good is God, one may ask. Just look around and see how people are blessed. Lok at your own life and know you are blessed. Because God show no favor to man. The poor and the rich are the same in the eyes of God. He gives to all. When I was a child my grandmother gave me a good life with the help of the Lord. I didn't always have but I had enough to want for nothing. I live in a shotgun house with chickens in the yard. And a chicken house in the back yard. We didn't buy eggs from the store. Big mom just sends one of us to the chicken house to get a few eggs and that what we did. She said it we did it. If a man doesn't wok the don't eat. 2 Thessalonians 3;10 for even when we with you, we commanded you this; if anyone will not work neither shall he eat. All man needs to do is listing to God, the problem with man is because he cannot see God, as he sees other men. He wants obey. But the word of God tells us in the book Philippians 2: 11 and that every tongue should confess that Jesus Christ is Lord, to the glory of God the Father, you can do it now are you can do it later. I see it better to do it now than later. God is the only one who give and don't want anything in returned. Man need to know God is not weak and He is the head. And He will always be the head as long as He is God. And the reason why He is God, because He created all. He knows all He is it. From A to z He the beginning and He the end. A man goes out and find a woman and when he finds her, he mistreats her and he do her wrong. And she gets tired of him he decides to he want to do right by her. Some woman tells the man she had enough and she want out. And she moves on. So, the man goes out and find another woman. He does her the same way.

This time he finds a weak woman. And he does her the same way. But she stays with him. He beat her some bad. She doesn't look for a way out because she was scared of him. Her dad knew she was scared of him so her dad went to see him and found him her dad told him to leave my daughter alone. The boy friend said to the father what you going to do old mam. If I don't the dad said to him just leave her alone or you will see a side of me. You never see before. And I tell you. You don't want to see that side. Please don't test me. At the end we both we be sorry. Her boyfriend said to her dad you don't scared me. The dad said don't let come to me again about you. You see the other side of me. Soon later the daughter came and told the father what he did to her. The father went off. And like a loin seeking prey he went out to find the boyfriend knew it her father the old man was all over him. He was beating the young man like men beat a man in prison. The old man beat him so bad that his gang banger friend put him out of the gang. He left the daughter alone. And set out to get the old man. One day the old man was coming out of the door of his daughter apartment and his daughter x boyfriend saw her. He pullout his gun and he ran toward the old man who was her father. But before he could reach the old man. A car full of guys saw him. They shot him killing him. The shooter was never found. Life lost. The old man was correction. And the guys who shot and killed the guy who went out for the old. That all knew the old man and they all like the old man. The old never meet any of them. He just saw them around the way. One night the old man was working late when he got off, he went to the club the night club to have a good time. When the club the old man name was bill. When bill left the club, he headed home. when me pull out of the club parking lot he notching a car following him bill kept on going home when bill got to the point to turn on the street that led to his apartment, he did not see the car following him. Bill park on the street next to his apartment. When Bill got out of suv and e walk toward his apartment. The car that was following him pull up on the other side of the street it was around 2;30 and 3;00 am in the morning it was pick black on the street and few street lights. And before Bill could reach his apartment someone in the car yell out to Bill. And when walk over to car he could see four black males setting in the car the drive of the car he was the one who yell out to me I turned and look at the car. And I said what you want. He said I want to show you something. I went to the car to show them I did not fear them. Because you show fear. You put yourself trouble. Never show fear. Because when you show fear the things you fear most are the things that come up on you. Whatever you fear it will happen if you don't believe that think something you did in the past. And you fear something may happen and it did. And if it did not happy it was because it was not in your heart. That it would happy. Did you know that before Adam? Disobey God in the garden of Eden. Man knew no fear. He knows no pain. He knows sickness and when Adam disobey God his eyes were open to all the sin of the world. The woman needed to stop listing to any man. And started listing to a man of God. I keep talking about faith. Because it is very important for man to live by faith. It was important that God needed faith to create the world. And with that man himself need it in his life. You may have money. You may have a home. You may have a nice car. And you may have good health. But it you don't have faith you don't have nothing. You can't even believe in God. Faith is life. We need faith all human need to have faith. Everything I do I have faith. And I believe. I believe in God, I believe Jesus Christ. Is God son. His only son. I believe.

This because God is spirit and no man never see God at any time. God is Jesus in the flesh. And He is God at the same time. Since God is Spirit, He could not come to earth as God the Spirit and deal with human who are in the flesh. So, God whip Himself in flesh and came to earth through a woman. And with God this possible. I don't think that God wanted to deal with man as the invisible God, I believe if man would have not sin. God could have deal with the flesh of and God would be the invisible God if man and woman would not disobey God, in the garden of Eden. When man did what he did. Everything would be change. With God and man. Both man and woman by during what they did meaning disobeying God cause human to suffer much. And man, still do not want to heeded to God word. It's been over 2000 years ago and man still understand that God are not going to change for man. So that mean man need to do something. And his ways. The time is running out. God, don't need to change. But man does. God been and He is good to me. I would love to see men all over the world sat aside a day and time the same of that day hold up their hand for 1 minuend and praise to God,

So much time has passed by now that I don't know what the date or day is. I don't know what time it is. I don't know how long it been. All I know is that I'm alive and I'm still breathing. I been having dreams about my mom. She has been telling me to get up and prepare for war but I'm scared. I been in the dark so long that I am afraid to fight. I know I disappointed my mom now but I just feel like giving up. I don't want to go on anymore. I have nothing to live for. As I'm thinking these thoughts, my body starts to shake and I feel rocks falling on me. An earthquake is happening and I'm stuck in between a rock and a hard place. I have nowhere to hide under and I'm basically getting ready to die because by the sound and feel of it, this house is going to collapse with me in it. A picture of my mom suddenly pops back up into my mind and I realize that this is the time for me to escape and take on the mission that I was put on the earth to handle.

All the techniques I learned on how to kill someone in 1.2 seconds comes to mind I stand by the door. I hear people running while the earthquake hit the second time, I wait patiently for it to stop. I know the earthquake damaged a lot of things in the house so I make a run to the door to make my escape while my dad is distracted. I know how to get out of this dungeon. How do I open the door? I must escape out of her. I must get out of this room? For some reason my mom comes back into my mind she gives me vision of a dark place with a wooden floor with a metal latch on the ground that leads to an underground tunnel. In the tunnel it has a bag with money, passport, I.d. credit cards, weapons, and extra clothes with a wig I'm guessing for a disguise. I don't know where this came from but I'm guessing the room I'm in has a latch maybe. So, as I lay on the ground, my hands are feeling for a latch. I'm feeling and crawling but I haven't found anything. I guess my vision was just hope for getting out until my finger runs over something sharp. It's the latch. It's so tiny that I would've never found it if I didn't have that vision. I lock on to it with both hands but for some reason it's not opening. I'm pulling and pulling and it's not opening.

I can't taster the fresh air and see some light finally but I can't seem to get it open. I feel around the area to see if it's a way to open it other than the latch but it's nothing. I wonder why it's not opening. I lay down to relax and try to calm myself so I can think of ways to opening it but nothing comes to mind. I take a nap and my dream was about a gun and a rose. I don't know what that means but I'm guessing it has something to do with me getting out.

So, I try one more attempt and that was to turn the latch. As I turn, it starts squeaking so I turn slowly to avoid any noise to have the guards watching the door hear. When it finally turns all the way, I lift up, then I see dirt and water. I put my head into this opening to look around and I see a long passage way with a flashlight right there on the ground. I jump down and turn on the flash light but cut it off instantly because of how sensitive my eyes are from being in the dark for so long. So, for a bit. I turn the light on and off for a little while to get my eyes use to light again. After about 5 minutes. I was back to normal so I made a run for it. As I'm running in this tunnel, I see no exit. Just a long way down and its scaring me because I don't know if I'm going the right way, will I be stuck, where am I? Just a bunch of things running through my mind. As I'm running, I trip. I hear my knee pop and I lay down to try to catch my breath. I flash my light around to see what I trip over and it was the black bag I seem in my dream. I crawl to it and open it. It was 3 guns a letter,

Some timberland boots, black jeans, shirt, blonde wig, black sun glasses, and money, credit card, I.D. and passport. I hurry up and change clothes and get the bag ready so I can continue but before I do, I open the letter. Stacey, you finally got this letter. It's time for you to take the secret and do as much as you can with it. I knew the day will come will this would happen because when I found out the secret, my days were numbered after I told you. Even though you didn't murder me, you father did because I told him before I told you. Do you see why you must not tell anyone? Remember everything I told you and read everything this letter says. After you're done, rip it up, and cover it in this dirt. I love you Stacey and I'm proud of you. Never forget me and understand that life is not to be understood, it meant to live. At the end of this tunnel, you will see the little light.

Push up on the top and that will lead you to a stair case, the stair case will lead you to a hotel back door. Go to the front desk and ask for Ron. Ron will explain all there is you need to know. He is your uncle, my brother, and he will always be there for you like he was there for me. Remember that I love you and don't ever forget me. Love mom. God help me.

People need to remember in order for God to help anyone when they ask Him for help man must listing to God voice. they must do what He tell them what to do we must go the way that God, sent us because have already put in place someone to help us. We much know that God work through people this is the only way He will help anyone. Through another people. He Himself when He wanted to come to earth. He came in the form of a man. And doing so man would upstand this was the way man could get anything from God, he must reach out to the man of God, God place man here to help other. When I speak of man I'm talking about man and woman. Everything God dose here on earth He does it through man. Before God could must get the approve from man. Genesis 1;26 then God said, let us man in our image, according to our likeness; let them have dominion over the fish of the sea, over the birds of the air, and over the cattle, over all the earth and over every creeping thing that creep on the earth.

When God gave man the dominion over the earth. He removed Himself and His author from doing what He want to do on the earth. God not going to give man the author over the earth then undermine the man. He not that kind of God, it is true God have the last say. But if man do what please God, then God will not change anything man dose. So many people forget about the author God giving men on the earth. So, they go around it. But God have not forgot what He did. God is so good that He gave the one and only one the devil to attack Job. Although was blameless and upright, and he feared God and shunned evil. Job 1;1. I don't think at this age and time. God would dare turned the devil a loss on a man today. I don't think there is a man like Job who feared God, and there is none who shunned evil. Not one. What you think would happen if God would leave man on plant alone with Satan. We all pray and think God for saying

He never leave alone. Hebrews 13;5 let your conduct be without covetousness, and be content with such things as you have. For He Himself has said, I will never leave you nor forsake you. This is why it is said. God is good and He good all the time. A few good is more than a lot of evil. Now you see why the world have not end. Thinks be to God, better then He who is in me than he is in the world, like I said before people think because God is God, He can do whatever He want to do. This is no true it is true God can do what He want to do. But He don't work that way. Any human who go to God, that person must first position himself so God can help him or her. We ask God for help. And when help us some of us never thank God for helping us. And we even praise Him. I believe when God help man someone will praise Him. When praise go up blessing come down. You may not praise God, but He will be praise. Aman. Why do you ask God, for help? Because you know He is able to do what you ask Him for. Try holding your hand up in the air and praise God. Don't worry who see you just do it. I remember one Friday night a friend and I was walking down the street. We passed by this build and that was having church in it. I told my friend my let go inside. We went inside he set on side and I set on the other side it other people in there. The preach was preaching. I could him looking at me and a few second later he said to me young stand up. I look behind me to see if there was anyone setting behind and it was not. He said it again. Stand up young man. So, I said to him you talking to me. He said yes, I'm talking to you. So, I stood up. Then he said come up here. And when I got up to where he was, he asks me if I was marriage, I told him no. he told me that God had a church for me. And it was a big church. He went to say that many who want to preach would has to go out and build their own church. But for me God already had one for me. I went back to my seat and said to my friend let go. Sunday morning came and I went to another church. The church was full of people. So, took a seat in the back. The church usher came to the seat and said to pastor do want to go up front and set with the pastor. I told her I was not a pastor.

So, I went to another church the very next Sunday I went to see what would happen. Just like before I set in the back of the church and the church came up to me and ask me if I wanted to go up front and set with the other pastor. I told her I was not a pastor. I left the church thinking. And I said to myself I would to another next Sunday. And would see what happen.

The next Sunday came around and I went to another church. The church was full of people over 400 I remember I was standing in the hall I look in the small window that led to inside of the church I was looking for a place to set before I went in, I saw this one space just enough for one person I went in and set in the space I saw. But every time someone come, I would look to see where would they go to be seated just a few second later I saw this little old lady walk in the church. And while she was walking, she looking in the area I was setting I told myself she can't be looking to set over here and just like that she down to roll and she made her way. And she set next to me. She said to rev. Are you peaching tonight? I told her I was not a pastor. She told me yes you are. I got up and I walk out of the church serve was over and left my car at the church and I walk home. Later that day I came back and got my car. After that I had a number of dreams. Here are one of the dreams I had. I was standing next to the wall on a bridge, I was standing there because the weather was so bad, I was using the wall for a cover to get out of the storm. This wall was part of the bridge that cross over a river? But while I was standing next to the wall I look and saw the water coming over the wall, onto the bridge, I got up and begin to move away from the wall, I end up in the middle of the storm and the wind was terrified. But in the middle of the storm there was a big white cloud in the front of me. I was walking up and down a road I couldn't see anything in the front of me because of the storm. And I turned and look behind me to my left I saw a tornado I feared for my life, I look for a place to cover myself but there was no place to go, but then out of no were a voice a planned voice spoke to me and said don't worry you are safe from the storm. Nothing going to happen to you.

When I heard that voice, I begin to walk not run, I became happy while I was in the storm. Because I knew the sound of the voice that was speaking to me, I knew it was the voice of the Lord God, I continued to walk in the storm and just like that the storm was over and the day became clear. This is just one of my dreams. These dreams have a meaning to them. What I don't know. But I believe God, will revile them to me. God is good to me. He always been with me He cover. 7 days a week 24 hours a day and most of all 365 days a year. And I'm not the only one He cover. We ask God He. But we do the same only thing. We don't praise Him enough. But we beg Him a lot. It is God create us. He understands us. But what if God had not created us and He didn't understand us that would be bad for us.

If I knew than what I know now how good my life would be. My life would be so much better. I do have a good life as I speak think be to God, God love this world so much He sent Him son. His only son. This is true love. And man say he love God, what if man love God just a little from his heart, and God see that. How much more He would for man. God could always do more for man. Weather man like it or not God, is the created of the world. He is who He say He is. And nothing gets pass Him. This is God world and before Him there was no man to Tilt the ground. Since this is God, world it would be easy for Him to say He done let the world come to it end. But He can't do that because of His only words. God word mean everything. He created the whole world. Everything God did He did it with His word. And He said.

Isaiah 55:11, "*So shall my word be that goes forth from my mouth; it shall not return to me void, but it shall accomplish what I please and it shall prosper in the things for which I sent it.*" God has sent His word out and many ways to do many things. Good and bad god gave the bad things it author. As well as He gave the. Good the right. And all He give He give it a limited. You shall the Lord your God, for it is HE who give you power to get wealth, wealth doesn't always have to be money. Long before the foundation of the world. Before anything God decide to send His word out into the space that He had plain for the world that He plan to create the world. I believe the world God word was here. It was God word that He spoke and the world came forward. His word is perfect. In beginning and His word is still perfect today. Then God said let us make man in our image. Who was God speaking about when He said us. He was talking about Himself. Because I believe the son, He was talking about would be Himself. He would later take on flesh of man in He come into the world. Jesus is God is the same time. For man tis impossible. But with God all things are possible. And for God to be God and Jesus at the same time He could do it.

If you don't believe that take a pin and paper and wright down everything about God. And then wright down everything about Jesus. And how much difference it would be between the two of them you will none so don't too much time trying to find any.

In the path that you are traveling, you will meet so many who think only of themselves and no one ease. We are to bear one another's burdens, without love where would we be now. The world is hanging on because of the love of God, the world could be glad God is good. We all go to bed at night. And we all wake up in the morning. And if you go to bed at night or if you wake up in the morning than you are those of all. So be happy. When things not going good in your life. It could be the way we thinking.

Proverbs 23:7, *"For as he thinks in his heart, so is he"*. How we think the girl in this story always saw herself in this way she was thinking. If this could happen to her. And it did happen. Man should be careful what he says and the things that come out of his mouth. It's just hit me that mom is actually dead. She is not in my life anymore.

I guess I am on my own. I'm in a tunnel trying to escape for my life. And my father is evil. I can't get weak now, all I can do is become strong and get ready for the obstacles I am about to face. I push the lid up and use my strength to pull me up. I'm looking around to see if anyone is around because I am on the run and no one is in sight. I walk with my head towards the door. She finds herself in big trouble and she needed away out. All she needs to do forgive her father. And ask God to forgive her. People want to hold something in their heart. And they don't want to forgive. But they want God, to forgive them. And it doesn't work that way. You forgive man. God forgive you. People find it hard to forgive. They don't care if its God, who said this. They don't care. A lot of things would be difference if man could see God, face to face. But man, much have faith in God, he must also believe in God, I remember when I had faith, I didn't even know I had it. I say it was faith because I went to cross this river. And it was a bridge that went over the river the rail of the bridge was about 2 to 300 ft high so I got on the rail to walk over the river. People in their car were blowing their car horn for me to get down so I would not fall into the river. It was a fool thing to do. I had so much faith that I believe that if I was in airplane and the airplane was some 35000 feet in the air and the plane fall to the ground. I would get up and walk away unhurt. And I really believe. And this is how I feel now. See I know God is with me. It takes a lot of faith to believe that. I have done a lot of wrong. And I should be dead. Many years ago. But God kept me here. If you are reading this book. You may feel the someway. When I was a young boy I hung out with big mom. We spend a lot of time on the fish lake fishing I remember the before we were going fishing, she would me dug so bate and I would. And early the next morning we got up and headed to the lake I love big mommy. She was fun to hung out with. I will never forget big mommy. She would always talk to the Lord. She would sing to the Lord. She didn't care who was around she would sing to Lord. She takes me to church with her. I will see he again. Almost all the old people I up with. They knew the Lord. And they believe in Him. This genealogy is weak. It doesn't fear God, it because they don't see Him many don't see and don't believe the invisible God it what He is. The word of say in the book of Philippians 2;11 and that every tongue should confess that Jesus Christ is Lord, to the glory of God the Father. In one day, our invisible spirit will stand before Him. Ready or not we will. Many have going and many more will follower. So, if you reading this book. Now is the time to get yourself together. Because when you dead it too late. Because when we die the only thing we can do is hope for the dead. I hope he with God, I hope she with God, that the only time we can't pray for someone. And God will hear us.

This genealogy is the worst of all time. When God decide to destroy Sodom and Gomorrah because was so weak and full of sin. This genealogy is weaker than those days. I have the chance to wright about shooting in the bar. How sad. For those people who lost a love one? How sad it is for a young person to go to bed one night. And knowing that would be there last night they would get to sleep in their bed. To be in house with the love one for the last time. It is good forgive everyone who ever did anything to you. You don't want to leave here having not forgiven someone. Don't worry about the person if they not willing to take your forgiven in their heart. And free you. You have done what God told you to do. And you are free. People don't care about other people. The best place to be is with God. And don't let nothing separate from God,

All I know is that imp happy to break free. I'm looking around for the front desk and I see it on the other side of the lobby. Behind the desk was 2 men and a woman. They seemed like they were irritated because of how busy this place of business was. The line to get a room was long, phones ringing from left to right, angry customers complaining and screaming, just hectic. I get in line and the man behind me is sniffing and making funny faces at me. I turned around to take a glimpse at him but he straightens his face before I can even turn all the way around. I don't know what's wrong with him but I'm guessing he is sick. Or maybe because he is white man and I'm a black woman. He doesn't seem to be that kind. You know what I mean. K.k.k. as I am waiting in line, the closer I get to the desk, I can the other white man say look at that black face the black monkey everywhere. I get nervous I feel the butterflies in my stomach, my knees buckling. All kinds of thoughts are racing through my mind. I never had any problem with a white person. Bu my dad did. He would always say the white man think he is God of this world. And the black is nothing. My dad was from the south. He was so far down in the south that when he grew up a black could not date a white woman. The white doesn't like the ideal a black man going with the white woman. That all you see now a white woman and a black man. And the white doesn't like it. This is why he believe the white policeman killed the black man. He is mad as hell to see his white sister with a black man. And for him to see his daughter going with a black boy he just cannot stand to see that. it hurt him to see his beautiful white daughter going with a black boy and to live and see her having a black baby. Because when a white woman has a baby for the black man the baby become none white. But if the black man has money it ok. It not really ok but he can and will deal with it. He believes a white man could never love a black woman. And he believes the black woman is wasting her time going with a white man. But you cannot tell them that. And as for a black man and a white woman. He believes the white woman is better for him than a black woman is. He says a black man take up with a white womanresute he is weak. So that make him a sucker for the white woman. The new game of sport is full with young men with black daddy and white mommy and they are good. They look white like there mom. And they play like they daddy the black man. God don't see no color why could man see a color. A man is a man. Don't matter which color he is. However, there is a group of men don't by that. He thinks he is better than the other man he lives with. That man has to be first in everything. But you God is good and when it looks like He not doing anything. He is all over it. I remember when my baby daughter. Was born the Lord told me in my spirit some with her was wrong. And later we found out she was born with autism I remember when we took her home from the hospital all she did was cry we didn't know what to do. But it was God who direct my wife in the right way to go to get help. And our daughter is much better. And she improves each and every day. She he very smart and she can do many things on her own. And without any help. She is a beautiful child. And think to God her mother is beautiful and smart. And she not like her father he is not smart at all. It turns out to be one of the smart things he did was to join the military. I remember when I got out of high school, I was walking around in my neighborhood with nothing to do. But get in trouble with the boys I told myself I sure go into the military. I waste no time going down to the army and I spoke with a person who was already in the military. I told him I wanted to go in the military. He told what I needed to do I did it and I pass the test. So, I was to go and come back the next day and if I pass the exam I could in. I came by the next day I pass the exam I was told to go back home and report the next day and be ready to leave out. I the day I took the exam the sergeant came into the test room and he told everyone to stand up. And I called your name you may leave the room. He called many names but he did not call my name. And when he finishes called out the name for those to leave the room. He stood in front of the rest of us. And said you all pass. And needed to do one more thing and that was pass the physical exam. I took the exam and I pass. I was the happy man in the world. Because I was going into the military. The day before going to the military they put me up in a hotel until the next day and we were told we would be leaving early the next morning. So early the next morning after breakfast the bus left the hotel for 7 hours' drive to where we were going for basic training. As we get closer to our destination. I remember setting on the bus watching the sun going down. And night was up on us. I got more nervous. And by time the bus reaches its destination I had calm down. And I was alright. They ask us did we want something to eat. Everyone said yes. We were led to the mess hall. We were feed. They gave us something to eat. And it was my first military mill. It was not that good. But I was hunger anything was better than nothing. I ate and went to bed. And the very next morning early in the morning someone woke me up. At that point my military journey begins. For the next few weeks I would be in Basie training. I had a tooth ache and the captain saw my face and he saw how big my jog was he wanted to send me back home and he wanted me to start all over when my face goes down. but I told him no I didn't want to do that. So, he let me stay. And finish my training. A few days later my jog went down I still had some pain. But I was alright. I was be hearing some devastating news in a few seconds. Next customer' the woman yells. Hello, may I speak to German' he is on break, may I help you? No, I need German now, it's very important will you or someone call him to the desk please ill see what I can do. She is so frustrated that when she walked away, she pushed the phone. I stand to the side to wait for my mom brother and I'm getting nervous by the minute. Behind me I hear so what! They can wait. I'm on break I can never eat around here. I can't wait till I quit; he was so upset to be disturbed from his lunch. He taps me and says can I help you? Are you German? Yes, who are you? I cleared my throat and replied quietly Stacey. His eyes looked like he has seen a ghost appear across my face. Hold on a second' he says. He goes behind the desk and does a few things with the computer. He whispers something to his coworker and he starts walking drastically fast toward me. He grabs my arm and tells me to keep up he need to make this fast. We walk up to the elevator, when the door opens, we walk in. I'm looking at him through my glasses and I see a tear fall. I get emotional but I can't let my weakness how right now. I don't trust anyone. My mind is trained to kill. So, I crossed my arms and wait for the elevator to open. We're walking through the hallway and I'm ready the number on the door. 426, 427,428, we stop at door 429, we enter into the room. All I see is white everything. This hotel must be fancy because the first thing I see is the big window with a view of the city.

All of the lights were just sparkling. Its shined like gemstones placed in front of the sun. The bed was white with fluffy pillows. There was a flat screen tv, a desk with a computer, and a love seat placed next to the window. I turn around and I see him using the chair as a stool to help him pull something from the attic. A black bag falls and its dusty. So dusty that the bag looks grey. He shakes it off and place it on the table next to the window. How are you doing? How are you holding up? He says. I'm ok I'm just confused as to what is going on, I sniff a few times to keep my tears from falling and sit back in my chair to get a good glimpse of him. Hess brown, with a rough tone. Short hair, almond shape eyes, skinny, and I can tell he is relieved that I'm ok. What happened. How did he kill her? As he wipes the tears from his face. He snapped her neck. I tried to help but before I can get to her, he killed her. What going on? Please tell me. What you going to do you black bitch. Take care of own business. I told him I was an off-duty police officer. I pull gun. And told him to get on the ground. Don't move. Alright you black monkey. I call for help. When the on-duty officer arrival on the seam. he asks what going on I told him. He told me I was I black police officer and I don't have the power to tell a white man to get on the ground. He wrote me up. He didn't have my back. When I came to work the next day. The captain called me in his officer and ask me what happen.

He said to me do you know the rules for the black police officer. He said they are not the same for the black officer as for the white officer. I did not believe what I was hearing. I told him I will never go by those rules. Those rules are not for me. I told him if anyone break the law. They will go down. And I walk out of his office and never looking back. The next day the chief brain called me at home and he ask me to come in and see him. He asks me what happen. He asks me to tell him everything that happen. And what was said to me by the captain. The chief told me that no one is above the law. He told me he would look into the matter this woman police officer had a brother. Who work for the Department of correction so she calls him and told he to meet her for lunch at the Houston restaurant because she needed to talk to him about what happen. When they meet up for lunch, she was telling him what has happened to her. Her brother asks could she get a picture of the cop who was giving he trouble at work. She told him to come to the station and he would be working the front desk the next day. So, the very next day he went to the police station. and when he saw the officer at the front desk. He knew him from the one he saw pick up a young black woman on the corner of central & 1 street. Her brother told her he was on his way over to his girlfriend apartment when I saw this black girl walking up the street. When he saw police, car made a u turn. And stop the young black lady. After a minute she got into the police and the police drove off the police car turned onto 2 street. But i went on to my girlfriend apartment. I told my girlfriend what I just saw what happen. And I went to use the bathroom and I look out the bathroom window. And I saw a police car. I saw an officer open the driver side door. He walks around to the back door. He got inside and close the door. I remained standing looking out the bathroom window to see what going to happen A few minutes I saw the back door open again and the officer got out of the car and he. Walk back around to front driver side and he got in. He drives out of the ally. I told my girlfriend I was going on the outside for a minute. I went outside and I walk down the street. And I got to corner of central & 1 street I saw the young black lady walking. She was crying. I ask her what happen. She told me the police officers rap her. I told her to call another police and report what happen. He told me that if I tell anyone they would not believe me. And he told me if you tell any you would be sorry. This was the same police officer who had rap a number of black women. While on duty. And never been charge with not one of them. She had called his chief and the chief told her not say a word to anyone about it. Because he had got a number of calls from other black women about a white officer. And he said he knew that the officer she was talking about was a bad cop. And that he had another cop to watch him round the clock. But that he has not been able to catch him doing anything wrong. The chief had told another cop what was going on and the cop he told went back and told the cop who was being watch. That he was being watch. So, the cp who being watch set chief up. With a hooker. And the chief fall for it. Not knowing that he being set up. The chief was on his way home one night when he got off duty. He drove by the through the city to see if he could anything going on. When I got to central and first street, he saw a black girl walking home from work. He pulls over and stop the car and when the young black came to pass by, he called out to her. And said to her come here. The black girl walked over to the car. He asks if any police officer has giving her any trouble. At any time. She asked him who are you. He told her that he was the chief of police. And he told her to get in the car. She got into the car. And right away he said to her you black nigger. I don't want any trouble from you. Do you hear me you littler black bitch? The city or the state don't need your king of trouble. What you and your other black monkey need to do is move on and go back where you come from. Do you hear me girl? Now get your black ass out of this car. And care your black ass home. I don't want to see you and my jail. For anything. And if I do you will be sorry. She continues to walk home and she meet her sister brother- law. And she told him what just happen. He called the chief and told him what she told him. When the chief wanted to know what the black was doing, he would get a hold Lee. Who her sister brother-law? But she never told her sister brother-law what the cop had done to her. so when Lee told the chief what she told him. The chief was very mad. So, the next night the chief went out to see if he could see her walking home alone. But when he saw her. She was walking with her sister brother-in-Law. The chief stops the car open the door and said to them what you folks doing out here. You're re name is lee I'm right. He got back into his patrol car and pull off. Lee said to his wife sister. I know him he not well. She told lee that he was the one who rap her friend. Lee told her to be careful around this cop. This dude is bad he is duty. This duty cop been rapping women for a lone time. I save his life one time he was going to his car when he left the restaurant and I saw to black man who pull out their gun to rob him and I stop them. I ask them what they were going to do they told me they were going to killed him. He is a duty cop I remember time he raps this young black girl and nothing happen the F.B.I. was called in look into the matter. He kidnapped the black girl. He raps her. She lost her newborn child. She lost her mind. She never was the same again. Her family wanted to kill him. But her father got sick and die. So, the family sue him but they lost. He walks away a free man. Lee was on the family side. But when Lee went to prison. This cop had a brother who work for the prison. Lee was sent to. To do 8 years for a crime. He did. His brother was let go. For having sex with a female prison. This is a family of men. who hates woman? They hate black people. Before Lee was sent to prison guard. he did he word for the duty cop uncle. His uncle was a sheriff One Friday even Lee was at work doing work around his uncle house and when he finishes work and it was time to go home. He needed a ride. The sheriff wife was going to the bank to make a deposit. Lee asks her for a ride to town she knew Lee mother. Because Lee mother took care of her house. So, she gave Lee a ride to town. So, when Lee got into town, he took the sheriff wife and rob her then he cut her throat he took her after he killed her to end of a back de end street, he left her body in the car. And he went and call the police and told them that it was dead white lady. In a car at the end of the dead-end street he said he did not know who killed her. The police went out and found a dead white woman in a car. Lee took the money he got from the dead woman and he went to a night club. After Lee killed the woman, he called for a cab to take him to the night club. So, the police headquarters call the cable company. And ask if they sent a cab in the arena were the dead woman body were found. And they said yes, they sent a car out to that arena the police wanted to know who was driver the cab and they needed to speak with him. The driver of the cab told the officer that he picks up a black man and he took him to a night club. Cross the river and the other city. The police ask the cab driver to take them to the place he took the black to. The cab driver took the police officer to the face of the man he drove there. The police took the man into custody,

They ask Lee what happen to the woman. He told them what he did, he said he needed some money so he rob her and then he killed her. Later the next night while her husband was on duty, he told the other officer what Lee did to his wife. He told the other officer that he was going back to the cell and hung that nigger and that he needs so help, so they went and hang him. Killing. And the word went out that he hung himself. The officer who rap the black woman. Came out and told the newspaper that Lee was hung by the woman husband and some of the other officer on duty, Lee family never believe that he hung himself. Before the police came to the night club to speak to Lee I was there when they came. Lee and some guys were shooting, a game of pool, and they were playing for money. For some reason that night Lee had a look on his face that I never see on him before. I knew Lee I was marriage to his cousin. The next morning, I learn what Lee had done. When Lee body was releasing his family sent his body to a place out of the city where he was borne. They were hopping they would a fear autopsy from a doctor in another state. The autopsy was the same as the autopsy giving to them by the first doctor.

His family still did not believe that autopsy. So, they paid to have his body sent over 1,800 miles and the autopsy came back. It was difference. That autopsy showed that Lee did not hang himself. But he was hung by the hand of someone else. When Lee was hung, he had hand cup on. But the police said that they hand cup Lee to bring him in. No cop was ever charge with Lee murder. They were let go free.

Sheriff Sayner ran for sheriff again he won. And he continues rapping young black woman. It got to point that more officer was rapping young black girl. The F.B.I was called in to investigation chief Sayner office. They start by talking with an officer who was clean. Some of the officer told the F.B.I that sheriff Sayner told them what he did with the black woman. and how they rap them. The F.B.I told the clean officer to go for a ride with the chief. And they should ride. In the arena where the black girl work Tell the chief he knows a black girl who he wants and that how much you want to sleep with her. But she always says no. So, the chief said to him rap the black bitch. She a nigger no one care about her or her kind. They all are just black monkeys. This is a white man world. Sayner when he was in Jour high, he had a run end with the black him and his friend was beat pretty bad. He told his friend that the black would pay. His girlfriend was beat up by the black girl. And Sayner dint like that. While he was getting beat by the black males Sayner was the football team running back, He was the star running back and because of the fight between the black and the white students the game was cancelled for two weeks. From that point forward Sayner never like another black person. When Sayner finish Hight School he went to college and finish college he ran for city sheriff. He uses power to lower young black girls into his police car. And rap them. For some time now, sheriff Sayner is being watch by the F.B.I and later that month he was seeing rapping a black young girl. He said he paid her for sex. But the young lady said no. and that was a lie. Sayner off duty friend went to the young black girl and they told her to change her story. Or she and her family would come up missing. So, you better change your mind and story. Or you will never see your family again. The girl told the F.B.I what happen. They her a phone recorder for her to record any officer who come to her. They told her to leave the recorder on all day. On that same night when the young lady got off from work. She was walking to bus stop and wait on the bus. To come so she could go home. And few minute later a police patrols car drove up to the bus stop. And someone yell come her. She walks over to the police car. And it was the two friend of sheriff Sayner. They ask her have you change your story girl. You need a ride home. Come get in we will take you home. She remembers that she had the recorder on her. So, he got in the car we should take you somewhere in kill you. That is what we will do if you don't change your story. Now get your black ass out of my car hold on Just remember what I told you. And what we talk about. They took her on a street where that way a gang street and told her to get out of the car. One of the guys on the street new Lee when he was in prison, he saw her get out of the police car. And he took her home. They didn't know that she one time live on the street they drop off on. She had on that street and of them was men. She was more save on that street than she was on the street she was now living on. From what I know about sheriff Sayner. He is a real ass o. he be this ever since I know him because of bad attitude. no girl wanted to marriage him. This one girl talks about the time she took him to meet her family. And co/work over and they were black. Sayner got so mad. And call me a nigger lover. I don't know he was like that but he was. I did not know he feel that way about black people. I ask around to his co/worker and so of them said Sayner hate black people. One of the them told her that Sayner once said if he could kill all black people and get away with it, he would and when he said that she cut it off. And never want to see him again. Because anyone who feel that way about another human, I don't want nothing to do with him. He danger. Very danger. I never saw him again to now. He never told me that he raps anyone but he did tell me if he could kill all the black people he would. The dam nigger black monkey. All of them is good for nothing. I'm so sorry I didn't ask about him why he was feeling about the black people. I just wanted him to leave me alone. I told my friend about Sayner and I ask them to pray for him. And that God would change him. The way he sounds I thought he would kill some of them. Sayner was a good guy. once upon a time. I hear about him rap the young black woman. Am sorry but I do remember this one time a black family walk passes us Sayner said when I become sheriff am going to kill me a nigger. I want to hear how he sound when he is dying. Now he on trial for rap.

I would like to say I am a white woman I wanted the people to know I don't feel the someway about black people as he does I don't any other white person feel the way Sayner do. Sayner x may not if he every killed anyone but he told a prison guard to have Lee killed when Lee was during time in prison it never happens Lee don't forget who set him up to go to prison. He told him cell mates who set him up and he told them everything he know about sheriff Sayner. One of the inmates had a sister who was rap by Sayner the inmate told lee when he gets out. He would take care of Sayner. And was for sure. This was the cop who put my brother in jail. He told the judge that my brother was a sorry nigger and that he was behind on his child support. He looking for the county to take care of his little black monkey. the judge said to him Sayer I know what you mean. But wish what you say. In front of me. The news what you did to the young black woman. I don't want you or what you ring doing to come before. I will do my job. What Sayner didn't know that the young black girl he raps her father was a rich man and one of the rich it. Man, in the state. Her father told her that he was going to leave her a billion dollars. For her and her baby. If she had one. Sayner didn't know the girl he rap was pregnant. And the baby was his. She didn't want to have it. But because her father had left enough money to take care of it. She decides to keep it. When she found out what her father did, she told Lee wife. And Lee wife told Sayner. Seven month later the baby was born. And she was very beautiful. She told her who her daddy was when she got older enough to understand. The child loves. her father. Very much.

She wanted to see her father although told her what her dad did to her. And have much he didn't like black people. The child was high yellow and she look like she was white. The child mother took the money her father left her and broth a home a nice and a nice neighborhood. She did everything she could to keep the child away from her dad. The child grows up her got her a car. On her 16 birthdays one she was coming home from school. When she was pull over by a cop. The cop was her father. He went to rap her she told him that her had told her that she was rap by a cop. He asks her who was her mother she said Sarah. He asks her where do this Sarah live. He asks her where did she live. She told him and he said how can a black woman live there. She told him that they just move there. He asks her where did you move from? She told him.

He was very surprising the woman he raps keep the child. He told all his friend and family about the child his daughter the 12-member juror found his not guilty in the rap charge Sayner begin to chance he turn his to God, he no longer calls black monkey and nigger he loves his daughter he was craze about her. But her mother didn't want her to have anything with him. One while Sarah was at work and Sayner was park across the street watching out of the place where she works. A little while later. Two men rob the place the men who rob the place told the police that were going to rob the place and then kill everyone inside he saves Sarah life the police told Sarah to come down to the police station to I.D. the man who rob her work place. And when Sarah got to the police station. The police were talking to man who rob Sarah work place while Sarah was listing the officer ask the man what there plain was, he told them that after they rob and got the money, they were going to kill everyone.

Inside. Sarah begin to think about what Sayner did to her. She forgave Sayner and she said to herself everything happen for a reason. When she got home, she told her daughter everything that happen that night. While she was at work. And how her father saves. her life. She also asks herself what was Sayner doing there. At her work place. She though he was there to rap her again. Like before. She told her daughter she could see her dad. She told her daughter to ask her dad why was he there. At her mom work place Sayner found which church Sarah went to he went to the church. And ask for their forgiving. The whole community knew how bad this cop was. But they didn't know he was Sarah daughter father. Did what her mom ask her to do she ask her father what was he doing there? He told her he got word that the place where your mom work was going to be rob. He did not know when or what day but he was there to stop the place from getting rob. But did Sarah and her daughter believe him. Both of them said they did believe him. For years, men been rapping woman and getting away with it but what know getting sex from a woman is the easy thing to do. There is much more woman than men. A man doesn't need to rap a woman.

All a man needs to do is let the woman know he like her at some point she will give him a chance to take her out and get to know her. But the man needs to keep his cool and not ask her for sex. But he should be patience and wait on the woman. She will come around. She already knows what the man wants and before she made a move to go out with him, she had already made up her mind to have sex with him. If the man plays his card right. A woman know that a man will do almost anything to get sex. And she has what they want all woman had that in her favor. She also knows a man weak moment is when he is having sex. And she knows how to use that to help themselves. And she not willing to give it up freely without getting out of it. it may look like she is but believe it she not. I believe this is why went she is rap it hurt her so bad. This is her gold mind. And she knows that I believe when a man raps a woman, he brakes her soul. And he rips he spirit.

I remember I went by to see this girl when I was younger, I didn't know she was a hooker we were standing in her front yard when the 18 pull up the man who was driving the 18 call to the truck a few minutes. she came back to me and told me she needed to go and make this money. She asks me to come back because she wanted to see me. I left and I went back. And when I got there, she was there she were there. She asks me to take her to a room. I said for what she said I want to make love to you. I told you just came back from making love to him. She said no I had sex with him. But I like you and I want to make love to you. With him it was business. My point is when a woman gives up her body it is for a reason. And when she is rap. It hurt her so bad it takes a long time for her to bound back and some time she never bound back. So, man should rap a woman. The same thing goes for a husband if his wife say no. She means no. But the think it ok to take what he wants and she hurt it don't matter to him. How many times this happen to the woman. This is enough to drive a woman crazy. This is why he go out and meet a nice man and she sleep with him. And she leaves her husband. This is why a man should never rap a woman. The women are out there to be got. And just because she marriage it doesn't mean everything is good at home the man needs to put himself in the woman shoes but he can't do that. But what he can do think about what he doing. And don't do it. He has a mom he has a sister. I had a girlfriend who told me she was rip by two men she knew. I didn't like then I don't like it now. It makes very anger just to think about it. One the woman maybe happy but the next day she may be sad and she would be anger with her man and with a good conversation from another man may all is needed to get her in bed. Or it may take a day or two to get you what you want. The cop who rip the young black women. He did it. Because he hates black people. Hate made him do it. Don't be like him. Use your head and mind in talk he into it. Sometime that work. You may end up lying to get what you want but you not ripping her. You know forget all of that. Get a wife get marriage. And do the right thing. Or be a yes man you can get all the sex you want. God is good and He should be parse everyday by everyone. At morning. at noon. At night. In the beginning of this book. If know then what I know now. I would have taking the other way. I would have done things much difference. I call my daughter the other day. We were talking and she said something that touch my heart. That hurt me. Very bad. She told me her mind was messing up on her she told me that she taking med. And it helps sometime. I left my daughter at a very young age she was ten years I just out of her life. My x wife who is my daughter mother and I was doing bad our relationship and out marriage was to the end I file for divorce and I decide to leave the whole state. My daughter and I were very close, we were always together. I didn't return home for minute years later. When she finishes school I was not there, when she got marriage I was not there, and when she had her first child I was not there. She went on to have two kid, I was not there. I was wrong for doing her the way I did, my is in her 40s and it beat me up to think about what I did, but think be to God for He that is in me then he who is in the world. My daughter and I talk more now. And when I go back home, I go by to see her. Life for her has not been good. Fear, but not good. I want the best for her and for all children. Never tell anyone what you going to do. But you should say to them if God is will, I will do always put God in your plans. This not what someone told me. It what I know. I have done so much wrong. But the Lord saw me through it. I know God is good. He good to more than me I know that. A man who has God that man doesn't need anything else. God been around longer than the world. He was her first and he will be around forever. I pray for the world all the time. I pray for people all the time. People I don't know. I pray and ask God to take care of them all, I know He hear me. He answered my prayer for He know my heart. I tell you get to know God for yourself. He is waiting to hear from those who are lost open your heart in let Him in He wait for you. although He God. People thank He can do whatever He want to do. This no true. God cannot do whatever He want do. And we should be glad. God cannot lie. God cannot do for man. If man don't want Him to do. It. Before God created the world, He set into place everything that needed to be in place. So that the world, could work the way He want it. God it a perfect God. This is why He say He is the same yesterday, today and forever. This why He said He cannot tie. Because of His world. What if God change His mind about things He has already do. Then He would not be a perfect God, He would be like man, and not like God, He said let us make man in our image, Genesis I;26. And what if God got mad. Like man get mad. This world would have been over long time ago and what if God love us the way we love other. What if He love us because we love Him? But He love us first. It makes all the difference in the world. Because when we Sin, He forgive us. This show His love for us. Man, love is if you love me than I love you. See God don't work that way. And we should be happy He don't work that way. When God created the world, He had workout how He was going to do it. He set everything in it place. And He gave them its power to do. Whatever it needed to do when time came. When I left home some 35 years ago. I knew what I wanted I also knew I would need the Lord is able to help and He will if ask God in the Lord name and you believe in him. I remember telling my dad that I was going to California. he asks where was I going in California, I told him to los Angeles he said to me why everyone go to California. They go to Los Angeles. I him why do you say that. He said you will see I remember one day I was driving down the street I stop for the Red light. And while waiting for the Red light to change. I look in the front of the car I was driving I saw this woman crossing the street and she was naked I mean she was naked. At the same time, I saw a police car coming up the street. It was going the same way that the naked woman was going. I wait at the Red light to see what the cop was going to do. believe it or not they didn't do anything. They just drove right pass by her. I could not believe what my eyes have saw.

Again, I was over to a friend house one night we were standing in his front yard. We heard some noise on the front street. We went to see what it was. It was a man and a woman fighting in the street. A few second later a police car drove up I told my friend somebody going to jail. My friend said to me they not going to do anything. While the police were there the woman pick up a pip off the ground and hit the man with it. I just knew she was going to jail. The cop asks. them were they finish fighting they both said yes. The cop drove off. He left them there. I could not believe what I just saw.

What it takes to be save. First you must believe Jesus Christ is the Son of God, second you must believe that Jesus came into the world to die for the world sins. And on the third day He rose and now He set on the right hand of God the father. If man believe that God is Jesus. And He is God at the same time and that man believe this from his heart. This man will be with God forever. Because God is Jesus in the flesh. God is spirit and the best way for Him to come to this world was through flesh. He could have come as He is and He could have deal with man in the spirit. The only thing be if He had done that how would they have crucified Him in the spirit to the cross. It is no way to nail His spirit to the cross. God is spirit and one never see Him at any time. When God came into the world as a man. And how we know that God is Jesus because it was God how said He would not share His glory with any one. And that mean his son. When God became man, He was a hundred% percent man and a hundred % percent God at the same time. Jesus was born with a mother but He didn't have an earthly father. Because He was God in the flesh. When someone told me that God and Jesus were the same, I didn't believe it. So, I went home and open my bible looking for the true. And it was he was right. If a man seeks for truth, he will get it. A man will always receive what is in his heart so seek the truth. And run with it. Help other and be help. Remember to do to other. That you want them to do to you. It is good to know what go around come around. It good that man should be happy I been marriage for more than 10 years and I have not been for then 10 years the last time I was happy it was when man set foot on the noon. i was so happy on a clear night I would go outside look up to the noon to see if I could see the man on the noon. If I knew then. What I know now I would have not done that. Even if the man was o the when I went outside, I would not have seen him on it. I never look for help when I was a young boy. It very few people I could go to for help. But I spend 17 years helping young boys and girls a volunteer's coach. One of my football players was killed in 1991 he was 13 years old. He was killed in a car accident. He was coming from church he was going home to see his mother. Before she went back to a rehab center for treatment alcoholism. When the car he was riding in stop for the red light in it hit by tow truck driver who ran into the back of the car killed my player instant. He never made it home. To see his mother the night before he was killed, he and I went to sport program banquet award at westside park to received trophies for his hard work on the football field. J. was a very good kid. He definitely wanted to be somebody, said C.J. J. coach he wanted to achieve excellence on and off the football field. C.J. says he had to literally drive J. away from the practice field every day. J. was a wide receiver, a corner back, a kick returner, he played everywhere, C.J. said and he wanted to be the best at every position. After practice, he would always beg C.J. to stay and work with him just a little longer. J. persistence on the field paid off this season. On Saturday, J. his coach and his teammates were awarded trophies during an awards banquet at kid park, coach C.J. was outside at the time and he didn't know that he had won an award C.J. recalled. J. came running out to get C.J. shouting, you. won coach of the year, coach. He was very proud. That was the last time C.J. saw the teenager. J. was killed and two other people injured Sunday when a speeding truck plowed into a car that was waiting for a red light at westside intersection. The driver of the truck, who police think may have been racing another truck to get to a disabled car, was booked for murder following the noon accident at the intersection. J. wanted to see his mother before she went back. To rehab alcohol house. On the very day my asst coach and I was standing on the outside in his front lawn when we saw fire truck, and police cars coming up the street. We continue to talk. But the next day C.J. J. coach was at home when someone knocks on his door. And a young lady told C. J. J. coach that J. mother wanted to see him. C.J. went to see J. mother. That when he learns that J. was dead.

A DARKNESS TIME FOR
A RELATIONSHIP

Weather she is an older woman or she is a young woman, she can't learn about a man quit enough just when you think you know him, he bright out A card he shed his real color. It just about to later. He has got the best of her. But the lady needs to know it is never too late. There is a good side and there is a bad side,

The good side is she didn't marriage him. That bad side she wastes a lot of time on this want to be man. He is someone who want to call the short, but he has not grown up yet. So, what that mean, he not a bad person not yet. But the woman needs to move on she should count her lost and head for the hill. And her next man should be that a man and if she wants a sure winner get a God-fearing man if he fears God, your chance will be good. She will have a good relationship. It not to say everything will be good all the time. It will not be. But it will beat having a worldly man who is lost. And he is walking in the dark.

When I was going with woman, I was seeking a wife. Every time. It took a while and a few relationships to find one. And remember stay away from anyone who is marriage. I promise you that you will before you get out of the gate. They already Belone to someone else. The wife I have now was another wife. I knew better. So, I went for it. This relationship has not been a good one. It been up and down. And we been together for more than 10 years. If I could go back I would. Some days are better than other. But it has been more sad days than good day for the both of us. We jump right into a bad relationship. I know it was wrong. I did not list to myself. My spirit tries to tell me but I was heard head. I got pen down, we had a child who was born with autism I could have walk out. And went my own and left her with our daughter. but two wrong don't make it right. And beside I love her I have won with this one. She is a good wife. I don't worry about her going out messing around with other men. She not a creator. And she doesn't lie and most of all she doesn't sleep around. I know I said she was another man wife. But I know her. By the way I did not say would never sleep around. She is flesh and she not perfect. I don't worry about her doing that. Things have been bad over years but she hung in there. Just like me. marriage for better or for worse. so, if you meet some who don't want to get marriage. Please don't waste your time with that person just move on. And don't look back. And when you leave take the time to thank God, remember there is someone headed your way. All need to do is make way for that person. Pray and ask God, to give you what you want. And mean it He will. He is able to do it. All you need is to have faith and believe. If you meet someone who marriage and they tell you they getting a divorce wait for them to get it. Do not sleep with them. And for the woman. A man think is he can get free milk. And why than cloud he buys the whole cow. If its milk, he wants. you wanted him help him make up him mind. Sex after marriage. The long you make him wait for sex. He will shit or get off the pot. Let him know you will not be use. Getting marriage don't mean you will stay. And if a baby is left, I can say it was by my husband. I don't want a man call me a girlfriend now that I am a woman. Let him know your girlfriend days is over. If you are good enough to sleep with. You are good enough to marriage. old school. Called what you like just don't called me a fool. I am trying to help you from making a fool out of me, and turn me into a scorned woman. A scorned have ugly ways. And she gets angry. No one wanted to be around her. Everything is all good because we have not had sex yet. Let him know that you can and you will get very ugly. If the time come. Let him know to stay away it will be better for him and mean it when you say it. Tell him not to push his luck because luck do not have a chance with a scorn woman and he can bet on that. Any woman can be a scorn woman. At ant giving time. Just about everywhere you go you hear the same old thing about men and that is men no good. He is a cheat and he a lair.

It makes no difference whether he is black or white. He is still no good. Women all over feel the same way about a man. They feel they don't need men for anything. But God don't see it that way. Man is needed for the world to continue. Women all over need to know this. If man so go the world. Man is God create. Women's in American spend millions of dollars each year buying love story books just to keep hope alive that someday Mr. Right will come alone and fill their love life. How to understand a man. Or what can I do to make my man love me and only me.

The truth is there is only one man and God create that man but there are many males' boys but only one man that man is a God man he is full of love he knows how to walk before man because he walks before God, he knows how to treat a woman. We living in an evil world it all about self. Nobody cares for other. It all about what you do for me. The only thing we can truth is God word.

We can always dependent on God and his word. He said His word will not return to Him void. That mean we can truth Him. This generation of people are evil. The word loves going around money. But it has no meaning. It easy for people to say I love you. And they use it to get what they want. People want love so bad and just hear the word love give them hope. The only thing about that is it the wrong person who telling them that they love them. We want to hear it from the person we love but God word say what good is it to love someone because that someone say I love just because you love me. See when God say He love you He prove to you by sending His son His only son to die for the world. John 15;13 greater love has no one than this, than to lay down one's life for his friend. Would you lay down your life for the one you say you love, and is they willing to lay down their life for you. I would say no but am no God, only God know man heart. It would be wrong for me to judges. Love is a strong thing. It because God is love. And everything He did He did it out of love. So, no man can say God love him and believe it. This generation has a hard time believing in God, and they really don't believe Jesus Christ, is the son of God, He is believed it or not but one day you will say it and you will believe it. Philippians 2;11 and that every tongue should confess that Jesus Christ is lord, to the glory of God the Father. You can believe now and get it out the way. Or you can wait. But you confess it. To die or live. To be save. Or not save. It would not matter you will do it. Most woman stay with a man and a bad relationship because she believes she can and will change him and when she finds out that she cannot change him it too late. She feels she gone to for to turn back. Now she spends a good part of her life hoping he will chance. And he never does. If she would have listing to God. It never would have gone that far. I believe before we Sin God spirit that live inside us will always speak to us and let us know what is right. Or wrong. And if we listing, we can hear Him speaking to us. All man need is the Lord. I knew I need the Lord a long time ago. I remember when I went to church when I very young. I would set by the window. I would look at the picture on the wall of the church. I would look at the picture of Jesus and the lamb that He was holding in His arm. This picture I dream about of Jesus one night. I had a dream I was walking around when I heard someone call my name. I look around to see if I would see who was calling me. I saw no one and the something happen a second and third. I look around again to see if I could who was calling my name but I saw on one there. And out of no were someone spoke to me and told me to look up. And that when I saw the face of Jesus looking down on me. Just because you don't see God it doesn't mean he not real. Where do you thing the world come from.

Some want us to believe the world created itself. It was God who created the world. If someone told you many years ago that when it rains there would be a rainbow will appear in the sky and it will remind of that God said He would never end the world with water as before. And some 2000 years later the rainbow still appears in the sky when it rain. How would this person know this after? 2000 years later. Only God would know this. Information. The things He reveal the things to man that man may believe Him. Am not standing before you telling you these things to ask for money. This is free information. You already have this book. I did not know you was going to buy it. Genesis 9;13 I set my rainbow in the cloud, and it shall be for the sign of the covenant between me and the earth. God us before the beginning of the world. What think would happen if man love each other as God love us. Man could never love the way God love us. I have always been in a relationship with women who was smarted than me. A woman is smarted than a man. As overall. I spent many years with inmates when I work for the department of correction, I would always talk to them about how easy it is to get trouble. I also remind them how hard it is to get out of trouble. It is very hard. If you lie you will tell another lie to cover that lie. You find yourself getting deeper in lie than want. The best relationship is a marriage one not to say all marriage are good. It will be problem there is so many people get marriage for the wrong reason. And for those who get marriage for the right reason. They too will have it trouble I like to say at some point in your relationship there was love between the two of you but something went wrong. Let look at the woman she wants to be marriage from the jump street and when a good man come her way. She is ready to say I do. And get marriage. On the other hand, the man is looking for a way he not ready to say I do the man sometime the woman know the man want out but she goes through with it thinking she will change the man I don't think it never too. late to walk away from getting marriage it better to walk away then to be sorry later. And have your heart broken. The consequences will be a lot to deal with if you go through with it. The man supposed to take care of the family. God words, you just my want call it God help himself plain His I believe God created the world He put His words in place and He gave all its power to rule the world and when He created the world. He sent His world out into the world to do what He told it to do. And no reason He would not go back on any of them. But He and He along to Change. it and the only reason He would change it would take grace to top it. For this reason, He told we and he tell us not to go to the right or to but we are to stay on the past. If God was some visible and reach to the moon and He was speaking to the world. His voice would put fear in everyone listing to Him, this maybe the reason why He sent His son through a woman. I don't this is the case. God is higher than the moon. He is a great God. But He do not have a stature. He is spirits. And spirits do not have a stature. I, am a regular man who have done what I know about God and what I believe. I hope it help someone. GOD BLESS,

A man needs to be reminded by his woman how much she loves him but if he cheats on her she will leave him. On the other hand, the man and woman need to let each other know how they in the relationship in the beginning of the relationship where they both stand on lying and on cheating. And what will happen when one of them is found cheating or lying. I can tell right now when a man finds out his girl or wife cheated on him, he will let her go. But sometime he will tell her he wants to work thing out. And that if she stays with him, he would do the right thing. He will her this to give himself time to think thing over. But at the same time, he has plans to leave the relationship. And if find out that she is sleeping with another man he will leave her. He doesn't want to think of him woman or girl sleeping with another man. He says have been the one who done wrong it will be hard for him to look at her. He could very much with her again but he will leave her. A man is like animal. He marks his territory; the woman needs to be clear very clear who she sleeping with and who she tells she is his girl or his woman. He going to mark her his territory. This is when some men turn to domestic violence and when the woman get out of line, he feels need to hit her. Or beat her. And man should never hit a woman. And no one should never put their hand on another person. When I work with the department, I was the facilitator. That one of my job duties to teach inmates about Domestic violence. Sexual assault. Child abuse. One of the things I dwell in the inmates' head. Was if they hit a woman or man. And they end up in count the judge doesn't care what the other person did he just want to know who pass the first hit. And most of the time it is the man who hit first. And all the judge waiting to hear. I don't it when a so call man hit a woman. I call a so call man because a real man will never hit a woman for any reason. This is why when a woman finds this tap of man she holds on for dear life. I let them know no woman like to be beat on. It makes. her feel like a child. A woman should never have to feel this way. I remember I was over to friend house. And my friend and sister got into it because she had something, he wanted from her and she said no he hit her so hard. He hurt her the sound she made when he hit her, I will never forget that sound my friend brother was there in the house when he hit her my friend brother his brother, he better no ever hit her again in the front of him. All I know he never hit her again. I told my friend brother he did the right thing. By telling his brother what he told him, where do the man get off hitting a woman in the first place. He doesn't have that right. Have another friend who one day he was going home and when he starts to pass his cousin house, he heard his cousin talking to this man and she was telling him t-out of her house but the man would not leave. So, my friend asks his cousin what going on cousin and she told him this man to get out of her house, but he wouldn't go. So, my friend told the man to leave. And the man still would not go. So, my friend beat the man. When the man got the chance, he pulled out his gun and he put it in my friend face he pulled the trigger six time but the gun would not go off. My just know that the Lord was with him during this time. Each and every one of us was giving a date to be born. And a time to die. And once this time come there is nothing none of us can do to change it. So, we will die and we will meet our created, this will happen one day. Many people know God is good. I will say of all the people in the world not one of them can that God never did something good in their life. But it maybe that God have not done everything they have ask Him. But God have showed His good to all. I say this because there is no way that God could good and showed it. God could not have this love and showed it. I remember one morning around 3; o clock in the morning I woke feeling some bad. When I went to bed, I was feeling good, but between the time I went to bed and 3.0 clock something went wrong my mom pass away when she was 60 years old my oldest sister pass away when she was 59 years old and my oldest brother pass away when he was 57 years old and had a cousin who pass away when she was 58 another cousin pass away he 60 and one cousin pass away in his mid 50s my point is I has so many family member to pass away in there 50s and 60s and at the time this happen to me I was around 55 years old and I let it get to my mine. That when I turn 59, I was going to die in many so case dead come that time of night.

Just because one believes in God it doesn't mean nothing bad going to happen. But the devil is a lie. When things go or going wrong don't give up. If wanted you dead you would have already been dead. And if the devil wanted to killed you, he would have done so. God let you go through things to help you to believe in Him, on the other hand the devil doesn't want you to go through anything he just wants you to not believe in God, and die a lost soul. Satan don't care about your soul. He doesn't love you. The devil can't love you. Because God love you. God love so much, that their room left for the devil to love you. Some people think the devil love them. I can tell you how good God is have you ever been in your own home on a cold raining night and you looking at T.V. and while you setting there you start to think about how good the Lord is and how good He has been to you. This is what happen to me right now I know what it feels like to have and I know what it feels like not to have. On this cold night I it takes me back to when I was younger. I remember when I was living in a three-room shotgun house, I remember one cold night around this time I was walking up the street going home I could hear the rain bounding off the ten that was the roof of the other shotgun house. On the street I live on with my grandma. When I walk in the door my big mommy asks me where I been, I told her round to my girlfriend house and was the truth. Back at that time we did not lie to anyone older than you. And you better not lie to big mommy. Because she had a way to find out if you were lying or not. She said they took your mommy to the hospital. And ask her why she said the man next door stable her because my mom and wife got into a fight and my mom beat him wife up so he pulls out his knife and went to work on her. My mom love to fight and call another woman a bitch. I knew I needed to get away from her before she would get me killed, I remember on night she was at the pool hall and her and a man got into it she told my cousin to come in get me. He did when we got close to the pool hall, I could hear the people on the outside saying hear come her son. The man she got into it with had left when she told my cousin to come and get me. I remember telling myself I needed to get away from here and away from my mother. Before she gets me killed. I was very young at the time and my grandmother didn't know what my mother and my grandmother daughter but back in those days you would honor your mother and father are u would get beat. And if someone call the police the police would tell the mom and dad to go on and beat you. It pays big time to honor who are over you. I was honor by the Lo Angeles police department and the southwest booster sports club here is what they had to say cub is proud to have Charles Johnson as a volunteer to the southwest sports program. Mr. Johnson joined the southwest sports program at its inception in March of 1989to the present. Mr. Johnson. Was given the task of Head Coach at Normandie Elementary School. His hard work earned his school a first-place finish in 1989, a first-place finish in 1990, in a first-place finish in 1991. Mr. Johnson is a year-round coach of Basketball, Football, and Baseball. His leadership in the southwest sports program has provided Direction, Education, Discipline, Counseling and a genuine concern for southwest youths.

The southwest police/Booster sports program has shown a great deal of success since its implementation in march of 1989. Briefly, this program combines services of the southwest area of the Los Angeles police Department with the volunteer services of the community. Along with the sports programs currently operating, counseling services are also available to the youths and their parents. Again, Charles has been a great asset to the Los Angeles community he serves.

This is just one of the letters I receive from our community leader wrote to me. I have many more awards for my volunteer services. Throughout the city. I have giving to the community where I live, I wanted to help the youth to keep out of trouble. I was honor for my good work and dealing with inmates in prison when I work with the department of correction. These was men I was working with I wanted to see them get out if prison. And have a good life. When I join the southwest sports program, my plans were. to be the best and I was the best. I wanted my boys to be the best. They were the very best. It's always good to be honor. Just like being marriage its honors men honor a marriage. If a woman tells a man she is marriage the really don't wanted to have anything with her. It is not to say he will turn away from her. Because he still wanted to have sex with her. Marriage or not. That all the man wants from her. the woman knows that. This is why she act the way she does. Her sex keeps the man at bay. The man wanted it so bad. He will do anything to get it. Know the girl telling her girlfriend what she doing to him. Before she gives him what he wants. Because she knows when he gets what he wants the game it for her.

Now the man calls the shot. She is in trouble. The man may hit and run now she hurt. Her heart is broking. The man true color come out. A friend of my oldest sister told me she said big red that was my nickname big red was the name the guys I played football with tilt today I don't know why they called me big red. I never been big. But you can say I was red. I was giving that nickname I have always had fear skin I was a light boy. the older I got the more my skin change it turn darker. I was o.k. with my skin changing. Because the man who was with light skin though he was better than the man with dark skin. He believes God gave him the Powell to rule over the other and when he found out that God did not put him over the other man. They wanted to killed God. But he did not understand that he could not kill God. So, they beat God son. And they crucify. Him but His love did not end there for the man. What man don't know he can never do enough evil to get God to turn His back on man. That just how much God love the man He created, the man Sin will always be forgiving as long as God has the last say so. And He will forever have the last say so. He is the first and the last. This mean He was the first here, He will be the last to go. Man should be happy that God is the way He is. But it doesn't matter if man happy or not. He will forever be the way He is. Like it or not. All the bad things and evil things man doesn't it only hurt the man.

The man still does not want to believe God created the world man need to get himself together and treat God the way he should be treated. When God took on flesh, when God took on flesh, He became 100 percent man. Before they crucify Him, they beat Him some bad. Although He was flesh, He could have stop them if just a word. He said His word would not return to Him void. This may be why God word tell us man should be slow to speak and he should be quit to listing. Since man was created in God image the man too is able to use his word in the matter God use His word, God gave man a lot of Powell to use when needed. But the man uses that Powell in every way but the right way. if man would let himself feel the things God went through man think he know when God son was sent to hung on the cross His flesh body was beat up. But His spirit was not hurt. His flesh body was cut up. This is what the body was for too pay for the sin of the world. The spirit of the body was place inside of the flesh to please God. But the flesh was for the man.

DEDICATION

I like to dedicate this Book to Lawanda, Charles, Shallotte, Porche, Charlize, may God Bless all of you. Because all of you have my blessing, Love Dad.

This is my daughter born with autism when she was born, I know something was wrong with her. I told my wife something wrong. I did not know that she had autism a few days later when I went to the hospital to pick her and my wife up. I remember from the moment I put her in the car seat to take them home. She begins to cry and when I gave her a bottler she would not stop crying. She would cry all the way home. And when we got her home, I took her out of the car seat I lad her down in her baby bed. She com down for a while. My wife gave her something to eat she went to sleep but she did not sleep long. She would keep her mom and me up to 3 in the morning. Before she would go back to sleep, I didn't know what autism was until my wife told me.

My wife knows she have other children but none of them have or ever had it. When she told me what it was, I didn't know what to do or say here is the story.

The story you about the read is true it was not easy to write this story because my daughter suffers with autism, she is a beautiful child she is not my only child. And she not my wife only child by the grace of God, my wife and I are able to deal with it. Being a child of God, He made the way for us to deal with it. And if it was not for the love of God my wife and me could not have made it this far. I myself was able to find some scriptures to help me in this difficult time. In the book of John 9;1-3 there was a blind man and as Jesus was passed by, He saw a man who was blind from birth. And His disciples asked Him, saying Rabbi who sinned, this man or his parents, that he was born blind? Jesus answered; neither this man nor his parents sinned, but that the work of God should be revealed in him.

Although Char wasn't born blind like the blind, man but I believe that God is going to do a work with her in due time, I know God love Char and He have a plain for her life that will glorify His name, already I can see the miracles thing He is during in her life from the first day she was born, I also believe that all children born with autism is for the work of God, though Jesus Christ our Lord and His only Son. Although there is so much going on daily in the life of an autism child the parents must willing and be able to recognize God plans for us and acknowledge who He is.

The bible tells us that God knew us before the foundation of the world, therefore since He is the one who gave life to all, we must truth him. Weather we are rich or poor. He is God over all creation. So, when thing looking down keep your head up and truth in the Lord, He said He would never leave us no matter what. Autism is a bad thing for child and our family to deal with but with our Lord, being there to help us through the hard time. Think how bad it would be if we have to deal with it all by yourself alone. When my wife and I brought char home from the hospital we through we were bring a normal health child home, we are blessed to have char in our life and we are blessed to have Char for our daughter because God gave her to be with us, my wife and I we both understand that by getting together that was the only way that Char would be born, therefore I believe it was us who God chose to be her parents and we thank God always, we know the power of God will heal her in due time. I believe God going to do something with Char that the whole world will see and they will know He is real. Millions of people will witness this miracle, while millions of unbelievers will be turned to believer and they will that Jesus Christ is the Son of God Char who is my wife we both Sin before Char was born, we also know God forgave us of our Sin. We know that God have forgiving us but there is a price to pay for Sin. And everyone who Sin will pay. It like man who go out and killed someone and the court send him to prison and the man was not save but after being in prison for a while this man found God and he was save so he turns to God for help. Just because the man become save, he still will need to do the time he was giving by the court. See God gave man the power to oversee the world. And court is part of the world because man is part of the court. And Jesus is head of man and God is head of Jesus. And no man or woman is above the Law. Only God stand alone. Because He the first and the last. God is so powerful that He put Himself under the law that He created. And God not concern about the things He over Him not because He is God. For He know nothing is about Him I have 5 children and I been talking to my oldest child about God. I pray for her and all my children every day and just the today 12/30/2018 she told me that she had found the Lord. She told me she went to church today. I was so happy for her and I was happier that she found the Lord. People listing to me God is good. But Jesus is the way. I can tell now don't go to God and ask Him for nothing until you go to Jesus first. Because God gave Jesus His son all the power in heaven and the earth just because someone cannot see God. It doesn't mean He not real. Man is flesh and God is spirit therefore man cannot see spirit while he is in the flesh. God been around much longing than man. Man is a Johnny come late. So, who is he? And that by itself should tell man he should do everything that God word tell him to do I am so happy it was God who created man. And not man who created God, this could have never happy this is why God is head and the man is the low. So, when Charlize came home from the hospital, I knew she had some favor with the Lord. And I knew she would be alright as I said before she is a beautiful child

Printed in the United States
By Bookmasters